The Elements of Earth

Poems and Illustrations

by

Stephanie Dougherty

The Elements of Earth
Poems and Illustrations by Stephanie Dougherty

•

Library of Congress Control Number: 2022912920
ISBN: 9781941573372

•

Design/Art direction: Simon Shendelman
Commercial Graphics, Inc.
commercialgraphics.net

•

Published by Damianos Publishing
2 Central Street, Studio #152
Framingham, MA 01701 USA
www.DamianosPublishing.com

Produced through Silver Street Media
by Bridgeport National Bindery,
Agawam, MA USA

First printed 2022

A lifelong hairstylist and a salon owner since 2010, Stephanie Dougherty studied art at Framingham State University in Massachusetts. She has received numerous honors and awards for her artwork, and bringing her visual art and poetry together is the latest step in her creative journey.

Table of Contents

LOVE
FAITH
PEACE

How This Book Came To Be

When I was young I excelled in writing and art –
The two to me could never part.
Later cosmetology became an outlet for me
To produce a livelihood creatively.

So many facts every day I learn,
Listening to clients, I hear their concern.
Life's experiences have been beautiful and hard,
Some bringing me joy, some leaving me scarred.

I sat down thinking one day,
About all of the things I'd like to say.
On society I took another look,
Then decided to write this book.
I'm optimistic that through the poetic word,
My hope for humanity will be heard.

The Bully

Trying to seem tough, you are so weak,
Hiding behind a destructive mean streak.

Full of gossip, fabrications and lies,
Your dark, hateful energy just multiplies.

Your friends feel protected, you're bullying him,
Until tables turn and it's one of them.

A bully can't be trusted, you see people as prey.
When I feel this bad vibe I just stay away.

The negative energy you put into hurting someone,
Don't you have a life? Why is this fun?

Isn't life hard enough without picking on each other?
Stop being a bully, don't prey on your brother.

S.L.Dougherty

Peace

What is love?
Does it come from angels above?

What is hate?
Will we learn before it's too late?

What is hurt?
How do you clean a dirty shirt?

What is war?
Haven't we learned from times before?

What does peace mean?
Or is it a word that's just too clean?

Decorating

It makes me feel like an ace,
I can live in a beautiful place.
Decorating doesn't have to come at an expensive price,
Creativity and a can of paint make things look nice.
For furniture check out the consignment store,
There for your money you get so much more.
Stencils and decorative painting can enhance,
When I do this artwork it puts me in a trance.
I want the windows to look sleek and clean,
Modern shades and shutters tend to be my thing.
For floors I tend to favor durable tile wood,
If water damage occurs it will still look good.
Bathrooms and kitchens don't always have to be new,
Maybe refinishing cabinets is all you need to do.
In the kitchen add granite countertops and a tile backsplash,
Pull it all together with colors that don't clash.
By choosing colors with artistic design,
Slowly your home will look redefined.
I feel like I live in a home that has been blessed,
A brush and a can of paint take care of the rest.

S. Dougherty

Control

Look how smoothly things tend to flow,
When you give up your need for full control.
Happiness soars when my spirit flies free,
Responsible, creative, light, and carefree.
I don't mind criticism when it's constructive,
But sometimes your control is downright destructive.
I'm not so sure it means you care,
When you dictate to me what I need to wear.
Style is a form of expression we can share each day.
Your edge makes me feel I'm being wiped away.
I see myself as someone who behaves with tact,
Yet you feel a need to tell me how to act.
If it's something constructive I'll listen fully,
But sometimes I feel you're being a bully.
You can feel how joyful our souls can flow,
When neither of us is in control.
We get along well as you can see,
When you can be you, and I can be me.

Discrimination

Each of us is priceless because we have life,
Ill-formed opinions cut like a knife.
There are so many things to discriminate against,
Just stop and think, does this make sense?
Judgements made on social class, age, and race,
So many obstacles everyday we must face.
Listen for a moment, this isn't funny,
Most of the world doesn't come from money.
Limited opportunities doesn't mean one's not bright;
Let the knowledge of life shine like a light.
There are judgements some people make based on age,
Maybe it's a time in our life to turn a new page.
All the wisdom and knowledge these seniors have to share,
Think of grandma and grandpa, the love, how they care.
Our genetics, not choice, determine what our appearance will be,
Yet such strong judgements are made based on what people see.
All this judgement around us, it's too hard to swallow,
We need people with depth, friends who aren't shallow.
Something important that we all need to hear,
Don't allow yourself to be controlled by fear.
To me the meaning of the word discriminate,
Means not to dig deeper, to generate hate.

S.L.Dougherty

The Narcissist

In the mirror you see someone beautiful,
But you fail to see your dark soul.
Manipulation and put downs, somehow your ego this feeds,
So hard on others yet so sensitive to your own needs.
So self-centered you hide behind an image that's unreal.
The victims of your abuse all need time to heal.
Putting those around you down in order to manipulate,
Taking away self-esteem, you are so full of hate.
Lying to others and filling those closest with shame,
When they end up with issues you give them the blame.
Everyone has to think like you to be right,
Otherwise sit back and expect a big fight.
When selfish choices go bad the victim you play,
Please save your sob stories for another day.
Why don't you take a look at your soul?
Too afraid you may find a dark hole?
Until you attain a realistic perception of who you are,
Those closest to you will keep their distance far.

Her Style

Her style is funky, colorful and chic,
A woman who has an artistic streak.

A sophisticated suit with hair softly curled,
She is getting ahead in the corporate world.

This girl is into casual wear,
Comfortable clothes, long pulled back hair.

Manicured nails, makeup perfectly applied,
This woman portrays a perfectionist side.

Different styles unique beyond compare,
We all must feel good with what we choose to wear.

Whatever personality type a woman tends to be,
There is a style within that must be set free.

Stefani Dougherty

Freedom

Have you noticed in these days,
Freedom is stifled in so many ways?

Life is a chance to be the best we can be,
The selfish nature of people seems to disagree.

Freedom should be a human right in our world today,
Yet so many groups want to take it away.

The evil core of humanity seems to want to repress,
Turning the lives of many into a big mess.

The voices of countless souls will never be heard,
Society is truly straying from God's word.

We must keep challenging ourselves to keep freedom,
Aren't we a step above the animal kingdom?

"Jesus said unto him, Thou shalt love the Lord thy God with all thy heart, and all thy soul, and all thy mind. This is the first and great commandment. And the second is like unto it, Thou shalt love thy neighbor as thyself. On these two commandments hang all the law and the prophets."

Matthew 22.•36-40

END
ST

What Goes Around Comes Around

Over time, I have found,
What goes around comes around.
I've predicted how the future would turn out,
By feeling what someone is throwing out.
A boss who mistreats employees may not get hit by thunder,
But sit back and watch while his business goes under.
I've seen people put selfish desire over their home,
Many years later they end up alone.
A woman who didn't treat her children well,
Years down the road her home wouldn't sell.
A man who taught his son to care only for himself,
Older and needing care, the son wanted his wealth.
Karma isn't aggressive, it happens over time,
It seems like a punishment for a spiritual crime.
I hope to treat others in a way that's right,
So karma doesn't come back around to bite.
Throw out kind words, an endearing sound,
Because that can also come back around.

Stefani
Dougherty

My Cat Tabby

It all started when I was young,
My love for cats had just begun.
Feral cats occupied our backyard,
Coy, cautious, and always on guard.
Bringing food and water, they came in a pack,
Carefully getting a feel for how I'd react.
I bonded with a calico named Tabby who had green eyes,
I sat and told her stories, we formed strong ties.
She kept kittens in a three-foot basement under our home,
At night I would hear them cry out, frolic, and roam.
As Tabby sat at the entrance, I asked to see a kitty,
She returned with a kitten so white and witty!
Seeing the outside world full of wonder,
When she put kitty down, it ran back under.
My cat understood me, I was blown away,
A memory I have that will forever stay.
Something terrible was about to take place,
Something permanent I'd be forced to face.
The alcoholic next door broke her leg later that day,
The Humane Society came and took Tabby away.
Writing this makes me teary eyed,
My love for cats has never died.
Why do sensitive artists love cats?
Maybe we're all just telepaths.

S.L. Dougherty

Colors

(I wrote this when I was 12 years old)

When I open up my bedroom curtains I'll tell you what I see,
Pink, yellow, and purple flowers surrounding an evergreen tree.

These colors add variety and life to our days,
And fascinate us so much in so many different ways.

People also come in different colors to add variety to this world,
But some are treated indifferently to others which is absurd.

Every culture has their own knowledge, talents, and ideas,
If we could combine them all together our intelligence would wiz.

Maybe if people could open their eyes and communicate with one another,
There would be no hate or war and everyone would love each other.

We should grow together like the beautiful flowers and make the world a united place,
Why must we pay so much attention to such a little thing like race?

Angels

After analyzing all the angles,
I stand convinced I talk to angels.
There have been many instances where it seems,
They talk to me through thoughts and dreams.
The visions angels send gives me a jump start,
To create spiritual images through my art.
Messages come to me truly enlightening,
I let them flow through my poetic writing.
Angels give vibes when something is wrong,
Open your heart, let them guide you along.
It's when I choose to ignore that soft voice,
This is when I make the wrong choice.
As long as I choose to treat people right,
Angels protect me throughout the night.
No one is perfect, we all fall apart,
What really matters is what's in your heart.
Warmth and love, a golden rule so true,
Pretty soon angels will be talking to you.

Things Come and Go

A memento mori is an image of a skull used to remind us
that mortal life is not eternal.

Thanksgiving weekend I was happy to get away,
off to Manhattan to see a live play.

Nothing but a good time was all in the plan,
some time off work to bond with my man.

Suddenly I received a call from home security,
I froze for a moment, what could this be?

I was told my condo had flooded out,
the floors were ruined beyond a doubt.

The next day I arrived home to the sound of loud fans,
as the insurance companies were all making plans.

The dining room table and piano were destroyed,
my adorable home which I once enjoyed.

I reminded myself that being alive in good health,
is by far more valuable than any wealth.

Material things can easily go astray,
my love for life is here to stay.

I reminded myself walking out the door,
this is what homeowner's insurance is for.

The Evolution of Humanity

We are introduced to a whole new way,
as technology hits our modern day.

Some will believe they stand a better chance,
when they use biotechnology to enhance.

Can this be taken too far,
will we wake up one day and not know who we are?

Is the controlling desire for human tracking,
achieved through the act of biohacking?

Things that make us beautiful,
some of it genes, some our soul.

Does cloning a person really go well,
or is he or she just another shell?

Another scientific endeavor,
technology to make us live forever.

I guess now nanobots are the answer,
when one discovers they have cancer.

Bionic limbs and joints are even stronger,
compared to nature they last longer,

How long do I want to live,
I guess as long as I can give.

Live, laugh, and love,
only with faith in God above.

S.L. Dougherty

Dreamscape

The sun goes down, it's getting late,
I slide into a dreamlike state.

My subconscious escapes with no hesitation,
diving into the depths of the imagination.

Suddenly I'm soaring in the sky,
telling everyone they need to fly.

I've hiked mountains made of multi-colored stones,
completely removed from all cell phones.

Swimming the bluest waters, they never get cold,
flying, swimming, and hiking never gets old.

Travel by train into a city to check out contemporary shops,
full of the most well-designed pants and embroidered tops.

Entering rooms with such creative décor,
I compare it to nothing I've seen before.

Everyone must use their chance to escape,
by entering into a dreamlike state.

Capricorn

I need to express what it means to be born,
under the sign of Capricorn.

Our earthiness cuts out all lies,
our humor catches by surprise.

Hard on themselves, easy on others,
protective of their sisters and brothers.

Being organized makes me feel whole,
to unleash the creativity of my soul.

No fear in taking constructive advice,
my personal growth I can't sacrifice.

In business I'm willing to put forth the hours,
love seeing employees blossom like flowers.

Remind myself of one big quirk,
there's more to life than just hard work.

Some say we're misunderstood,
in my opinion it's all good.

Due to the day and month in which I was born,
I was destined to be a Capricorn.

My Cat Flies

Flying high and looking pretty,
in the sky, that's my kitty.

I turn around,
he's off the ground.

With all his might,
he takes flight.

Avoiding gravity's pull,
he's clearly a real soul.

In the air within minutes,
I swear my cat knows no limits.

I stand in awe,
he spreads his paw.

On the desk, gliding through folders,
next thing I know he's on my shoulders.

Up, up, and away,
I experience this every day.

It's a bird, it's a plane, no that's my cat,
up in the air is where he's at.

California

The thing I remember to this date,
visiting California, The Golden State.

Touring San Francisco in all of it's glory,
Alcatraz and The Golden Gate both tell a story.

Few things ever felt so jolly,
as hopping on the city's trolley.

Seeking nature as nourishment for the soul,
embracing Muir Woods and Old Faithful.

Traveling down south, somewhat far,
maybe I'll be a Hollywood star.

Go to the beach, lay out in the sand,
experience the magic of Disneyland.

Driving south is a vast desert fighting to survive,
high temperatures are what keep this land alive.

Snakes, lizards, the Joshua Tree,
rainfall is an anomaly.

Crowded with cactus, tumbleweeds turning,
perfects the environment for wildfires burning.

Not only remembered for fires and palm trees,
but also well known for the expensive fees.

These rising California prices,
contribute to the homeless crisis.

This diverse landscape is notably breathtaking,
sculpted by San Andreas Fault Line shaking.

Not knowing whether to sink or sail,
scoring high on the Richter Scale.

No way of knowing when this land will give,
California might be the place to visit, not to live.

Boston

Of the cities to visit that should not be missed,
Boston, Massachusetts should place in this list.

During 1690 it was Puritan founded,
it's earned a reputation for being grounded.

Leading the country for education and art,
those who reside here are viewed as smart.

Schools for the gifted with a high IQ,
Harvard and Tufts to name a few.

For the more hands on what's really cool,
NBSS, America's first trade school.

Students taught refined skills, learning to thrive,
giving life meaning, new ways to survive.

Famous for so many things,
please don't forget Boston's baked beans.

During 1897 the United States was elated,
in Boston the first subway system was created.

Eager to see things that make my mind grow,
the Museum of Science steals the show.

Outside boards the duck tour, a journey through water and land,
a sightseeing expedition that couldn't have been better planned.

Park Ferry to Boston Islands for the day,
seeing the area in a whole new way.

Inspiring musicians on a late night out,
is what the symphony orchestra is all about.

During spring and summer spending sensual hours,
embracing Botanical Garden's colorful flowers.

Walking among the warm leaves of autumn,
over the bridge of the Boston Common.

Note on the list, a sure must see,
Boston for innovation and diversity.

Confusion

Puzzled by the illusions of life,
confusion cuts me like a knife.

Society teaching us who to be,
through this maze it's hard to see.

Sometimes I wish I had attended more school,
afraid others will view me as a fool.

To stop my self-esteem from becoming a mess,
I remind myself to define success.

Working on something I've desired,
means more to me than money acquired.

Marriage has been pushed as part of the plan,
implying a woman's strength is in a man.

Allowing relationships to go on too long,
this, I believe, is where I went wrong.

I'll stick to playing to the beat of my own drum,
staying with the wrong person only seems dumb.

More than relationships or any wealth,
are the reflections of my feelings toward myself.

Finding my way, following a new direction,
defying the laws of natural selection.

Parting from society makes me feel whole,
no longer a person, truly a soul.

I've stopped living the lie of social illusion,
relying on my inner blade to cut the confusion.

S.L. Dougherty

Marine Heaven

While deep sea diving through an underwater Mars,
amazed by an aquatic heaven with oceanic stars.

The sea bottom, a deepest dark night,
life evolving here can produce its own light.

Aquatic plants provide oxygen, shelter, and food,
this world of serene lifeforms tranquilizes my mood.

A school of multi-toned fish cautiously gliding,
provides camouflage, illusion, a way of hiding.

With complicated sounds, whales converse,
amongst one another is where they rehearse.

Sea turtles can take a strong dive in an instance,
into deep depths and swim quite the distance.

In shallow tropical and temperate waters seahorses wait,
to find themselves a lifetime mate.

All these creatures of the sea,
communicate, exude personality.

Not only do they spread their ocean wings,
many can do amazing things.

The octopus clambering over rocks in shallow zones,
are able to shift their color to a variety of tones.

Nothing regenerates body parts faster,
than the renowned, smiling alabaster.

Jellyfish, the oldest organism alive,
water is where they learned to survive.

These marine life forms are just a few examples,
scientists continue searching the ocean for samples.

Only five percent of these waters have been explored,
so rumors of sightings can't go ignored.

The giant squid, a species of deep ocean dwelling,
can it take down a ship, there's no way of telling.

If a tidal wave comes and takes me away,
maybe a mermaid will come save the day.

Making me part of these heavenly waters,
a place where I can float and glide for hours.

Girls' Night Out

Those with compassion are welcome to take part,
understanding others' needs is a developing art.

Quick to listen and nurture, cautiously holding back,
we are here to be joyful, no need to attack.

Variety is the herb that gives life spice,
all that is diverse makes living nice.

Time spent to encourage each other is what this evening is about,
women around the world are all invited to Girls' Night Out.

Wisdom

As experience, judgement, and knowledge unfold,
wisdom becomes worth its weight in gold.

A wise person never thinks twice,
when paying attention to sound advice.

By listening to what others know,
intellectually we continue to grow.

Whether it be a budget, business, or plan of any size,
discipline is used when a person is wise.

Many are driven by materialistic needs,
accumulating debt, living beyond their means.

Money, a substance that can come and go,
better to save, not to owe.

Other people's actions one cannot control,
the power of wisdom comes from the soul.

Humbly accepting constructive instruction,
at a higher level the wise will function.

Every move signed and dated,
every risk calculated.

Questioning if this is real rejection,
or is this area not my section.

Dependability is always a must,
as important, worthy of trust.

Earned the reputation of rock-solid agents,
handling tough situations with a lot of patience.

Cautiously choosing the words from their lips,
the wise form solid relationships.

Building up others to feel like stars,
breaking down cultural bars.

A wise person isn't at all fake,
quick to own up to an honest mistake.

There is no reason to hide,
when wisdom is the guide.

There is no color that can disguise,
the golden aura surrounding the wise.

Customer Service

It's important to make your service the best,
Warmth, love, and kindness take care of the rest.

As imperative as quality is the human touch,
Sensitivity towards others just means so much.

If the focus is money, you'll never have enough to live,
If the focus is your best with love, there will be money to give.

There's a gar-den, what a gar-den, On-ly hap-py fa-ces bloom there
LOVE
JOY
PEACE
HAPPY
CARING
GIVE
THANKFUL
S.L. Dougherty

Love

Images of butterflies joyful and free,
this is the vision love sends to me.

Like a symphony that performs from above,
I hope to express the melody of love.

Humility is a trait that's not learned in college,
mistakes, with love, one will quickly acknowledge.

A heart of love urges humanity to learn,
the art of giving without getting in return.

Even when one has a lot at stake,
selfless sacrifices love will make.

Always looking for ways to give,
delicate, kind, and sensitive.

A soil that nurtures nutritional flow,
a heart of forgiveness allows others to grow.

Protect the privacy of sisters and brothers,
love must resist backstabbing others.

On the joy and growth of others is where love feeds,
so whole and complete, love has no needs.

A cheerful heart that's positive,
a trait pure love is sure to give.

A heartfelt soul quickly encourages a friend,
we've all had times we need a hand.

Wise and mature, love is discreet,
helping others get on their feet.

As the butterfly comes in for a landing,
my heart floods over with understanding.

Respectful when someone views life different than me,
individuality, the inner soul that sets us free.

Full of gratitude for a chance at living,
my heart, mind, and soul are filled with thanksgiving.

Whether one may win or lose,
love is happy in his own shoes.

Love teaches us to grow we must,
over time develop trust.

Through life's episodes of great sorrow,
love is our hope for a brighter tomorrow.

Love is the only place to start,
we are strong together, not apart.

When the hearts of humanity are set aglow,
it is in this environment love will flow.

As diverse as the butterflies feeding off flowers,
love, the condition that endures endless hours.

Love is the universal melody that bring with it a synergy,
megahertz of hope, passion, excitement, and energy.

My Morning Drive

Allowing positive thought to thrive,
freeing my mind on a morning drive.

Healing the World
Challenges
Worthy of Happiness
Setting Boundaries
My Own Hero
Unshaken
The Joy of Doing Nothing
Attention on Healing
Always in the Right Place
Perfection Perception
Negative Emotions
Bubble of Love
Struggle to Believe
Giving Each Other Space

Gratitude

During life's challenges I choose to take part,
taking steps towards attaining a grateful heart.

Avoid putting the focus on things that are wrong,
acknowledgement of blessings should guide us along.

For every helpful gift show thanksgiving,
giving back to others gives reason for living.

Alive in a world that is full of sorrow,
always keep hope for a brighter tomorrow.

Sometimes it seems life's unfair,
keep your thoughts on those who care.

When it comes to others we have no control,
over the hidden demons surrounding their soul.

Fill our lives with helping hands,
selectively choosing our own friends.

Instead of self-criticism, learn from situations,
put forth your energy to build good relations.

Stay away from those who have done you wrong,
cut the binding chains and sing a free song.

During all of life's hardships, steadfast I strive,
through good judgement and hard work, I know I'll survive.

Sharing positive stories, please let them be heard,
reminding us all of the good in this world!

There is nothing I could say or do,
to show how grateful I am for you.

I will continue to widen my inner latitude,
and let it overflow with so much gratitude.

NEW RENAISSANCE POEMS

Religious Definition

Long ago I made the decision,
to no longer be defined by religion.

Some try to convey how good they are,
by a cross, a veil, or Judaic star.

True spirituality is shown by the way,
one treats other people every day.

Religious institutions all have their place,
if they don't make changes challenges they face.

Some of these leaders give the guidance of fools,
encouraging submission to man-made rules.

Dictating to people how to dress,
insisting in the need to confess.

Is confession really God's way?
you mean I, myself, cannot pray?

People told that to obey your master,
give money to church and heaven comes faster.

What comes to me when I pray,
give where there are needs every day.

Does it give the church a stronghold,
if they can pack me into a mold?

Trying to guide my spiritual expression,
throwing me into a state of depression.

Unconvinced this is concern for my soul,
feels more to me like full control.

Claiming to love God, or so they say,
some were members of the KKK.

Some governments choose to break the silence,
using religion as an excuse for violence.

During the Spanish Inquisition people were tortured for thinking,
this is enough to drive a man to drinking.

In the Middle East leaders have ordered countless killing,
I guess to someone's ego this was fulfilling.

Centuries of genocides and religious feasts,
bloodshed in the Middle East.

India had a caste system impossible to rise above,
about control and repression, excluding love.

These are just a few examples of religious drama,
inflicting on millions of lives so much trauma.

Through religious abuse, so many cry,
true guarantee, one day we all die.

Was I the person I wanted to be,
love, compassion, honesty?

When it's all over to me what matters,
did I live a life that flatters.

Spirituality when used in the right way,
peace and understanding will convey.

It has become my diverse opinion,
God's people are born into all religions.

God must look at society with unwavering sorrow,
so full of hatred, will there be a tomorrow?

I believe the Lord in heaven must be looking down,
upon some of these institutions wearing a frown.

Forgive

Sometimes I feel down about what I see,
The way people treat others and what's on TV.
It seems no one cares at all about life,
The environment, endangered species, human strife.
If we could treat our neighbor as our brother,
Break down the walls and love one another.
Is it possible to put away our fear?
Celebrate differences from year to year?
The world would be an ideal place to live,
If we find in our hearts a place to forgive.

S.L.
Dougherty

Dear Mom, I Love You

Sincerely, Stephanie

Though at times it seems untrue,
Mom, I really do love you.

If at times I seem upset,
those three words you won't forget.

Any time I need a friend,
you're always there, you understand.

Believe me, it's really true,
I just can't live without you.

CLEOCATRA
NEFERKITTY

The History of Cats

Cats have resided with humans for thousands of years,
to some cultures worshipped, to others brought fears.

It was decided 10,000 years ago the cat could stay,
great for keeping the mice away.

Cats with docile traits were preferred,
over time they became revered.

In ancient Egypt, royalty, dressed in jewels,
never abiding by laws or rules.

Cunning, magical, and smart,
Egypt is filled with feline art.

Statues and paintings of every breed,
a warm-hearted cat for some fill a need.

Bringing good fortune to a home,
no control over where they roam.

In Beni-Hassan there is a cemetery where dead cats reside,
over 3,000 and counting were mummified.

Anyone who killed a cat received the death sentence,
for this crime there was no repentance.

From gods to demons over hundreds of years,
during the Middle Ages cats brought great fears.

To ward off evil, cats were demonized and killed,
the death of thousands takes time to rebuild.

After this mass genocide, it didn't take long,
for Europeans to realize that they were wrong.

Because of this war against innocent cats,
the Bubonic Plague was able to spread through rats.

During the 1600s cats' image rose in the west,
for sensitive artists, the cat was the best.

As close to perfection an animal can get,
considered by many the perfect pet.

Cuddly, independent and strong,
with a cat one can't go wrong.

Nobody can tell a cat where to roam,
still always in question who owns this home.

JOY
PEACE
FAITH
S.L. Dougherty

Real Beauty

The traits that make one beautiful,
qualities coming straight from the soul.

Quick to listen, help someone learn,
demanding nothing in return.

Searching to see the positive side,
sincere and honest, nothing to hide.

Joyful, intelligent, and capable,
within themselves they are whole.

Low on pride, high on humility,
understanding is the key.

Always eager to learn and grow,
an aura of compassion makes them glow.

Using their gifts to bring others light,
finding solutions to a potential fight.

We all have talents that must come out,
sharing with the world what life is about.

Wisdom, courage, kindness, and love,
coming in for a landing, white as a dove.

Others needs beauty sees,
generously involved in charities.

Slow to judge others, quick to embrace,
loves every social class, gender, and race.

Staying positive, fighting their way through this world,
with the promise hope for humanity will one day be heard.

Gratitude for all that you have, showing thanksgiving,
Everything that surrounds us gives reason for living.

Dougherty

Inner Strength

Driving through life's stormy weather,
full of hope that things will get better.

During life's challenges it doesn't take long,
to realize the importance in staying strong.

Mindfulness, resilience, and empathy,
are the emotional skills that set us free.

With love, compassion, and gratitude,
positive energy we will exude.

Keeping a humorous, responsible, relaxed manner,
on the inside sporting a metal banner.

Generous, hardworking, and wise,
warm hearts free from society's lies.

Strength to keep going after rejection,
mentally winning every election.

Striving to be forgiving,
with purpose goes on living.

Don't allow fear to take over decisions,
brave as a fighter pilot in my visions.

Leave past hurts behind,
become a legend of the mind.

Standing by what feels right,
listening to that inner light.

When others try to break your soul,
a thick skin resists this negative pull.

Set all expectations high,
know the limit is the sky.

S.L.
Dougherty

The Joys of Spring

Nature transforms from cold and gray,
color emerges wiping winter away.

Spring's cheerful daffodils flower about,
hedgehogs and dormice start to come out.

A chorus of birds singing just before dawn,
blue, pink, and burgundy brighten the lawn.

Bumblebees in flight swarm around flowers,
finding their nest site in a matter of hours.

A kaleidoscope of butterflies fluttering free,
the drumming of a woodpecker tapping a tree.

Deer come out with the grass and trees,
attracting attention from ticks and fleas.

Bluebells cover the grounds in a soft blue haze,
offering the woodlands a tranquil new glaze.

Barren winter trees are soon to be seen,
sporting a refreshing new shade of green.

All of nature is starting to sing,
a song that is filled with the joys of spring.

Family

The bond goes deeper than skin, eyes, and hair,
what makes a family are people who care.

Going beyond a similar face,
with love they offer a warm embrace.

Gifts and talents passed down generations,
support and protection on all occasions.

Finding ways to gather, no matter the weather,
working on situations pulling together.

Ethics and values form a connection,
members allowed their own direction.

Positive communication is always a must,
having strong boundaries also builds trust.

Family enforces that if we have hope,
through life's challenges we will cope.

Patience, honesty, courage, compassion,
qualities that never go out of fashion.

Adaptable, self-disciplined, kindness towards others,
quick to encourage sisters and brothers.

Humility, contentment, and determination,
guides a family through any situation.

Dependability is a must,
as is honesty, worthy of trust.

Teach your kids to stay away,
from putting off for tomorrow what can be done today.

Sometimes you must follow, sometimes you lead,
full of gratitude and respect as you proceed.

During life's hardships families must endure,
allow lots of optimism to be the cure.

As the years go by stay eager to learn,
knowledge, the key that helps us discern.

Molding children with integrity, ethics, and love.
will be smiled upon by the Lord above.

Self-Criticism

If self-criticism is getting you down,
look for a way to turn it around.

Instead of setting standards too high,
exude patience, give your best try.

With practice continue to move,
over time you will improve.

Learn skills slowly, get help from a friend,
support, encouragement, a helping hand.

Perfection doesn't come overnight,
slow and steady does the job right.

In certain areas some are more gifted,
use your gifts to make others uplifted.

Stop harsh mental talk, this does no good.
instead of I can't, start thinking I could.

When given the time to reflect,
we have life, we're all perfect.

Instead of filling your mind with harsh mental talk,
think positive thoughts and in light you will walk.

A Time for Everything

Ecclesiastes 3:1-8

There is a time for everything,
and a season for every activity under the heavens:

a time to be born and a time to die,
a time to plant and a time to uproot,

a time to kill and a time to heal,
a time to tear down and a time to build,

a time to weep and a time to laugh,
a time to mourn and a time to dance,

a time to scatter stones and a time to gather them,
a time to embrace and a time to refrain from embracing,

a time to search and a time to give up,
a time to keep and a time to throw away,

a time to tear and a time to mend,
a time to be silent and a time to speak,

a time to love and a time to hate,
a time for war and a time for peace.

Wise Words to Consider

Jesus said unto him, "Thou shalt love thy God with all thy heart, all thy soul, and all thy mind. This is the first and greatest commandment.

And the second is like unto it: Thou shalt love thy neighbor as thyself. On these two commandments hang all the law and the prophets."

Matthew 22:37-40

Finally, brethren,
whatever things are true, honest, just, pure, lovely, of good report; think on these things.

Philippians 4:8

Earth's Elements

Lightning strikes, full of desire,
igniting into a flame of fire.

The wind whips up, offering a hand,
flames given the chance to encircle the land.

The air now traveling at record speed,
strengthens the fire's raging need.

With vengeance, burning into a wave of flame,
devouring everything, there is no shame.

The day turns to night, the clouds settle in,
now heavy rainfall has the chance to begin.

As water pours down, the puddles get higher,
surrounding and defeating the deadly fire.

Land full of ashes, plantation destroyed,
once there was beauty, now there's a void.

The sun rises providing life to all,
to the sound of a bubbling waterfall.

A gentle breeze blowing with care,
again serenity fills the air.

Solid earth exudes resilience from attack,
in no time at all vegetation grows back.